PISSARRO

Pissarro

by Raymond Cogniat

CROWN PUBLISHERS, INC. - NEW YORK

Title page: PORTRAIT OF THE ARTIST, 1873
Oil, 22" x 18 1/8"
Jeu de Paume Museum, Paris

Translated from the French by:
ALICE SACHS

Collection published under the direction of:
MADELEINE LEDIVELEC - GLOECKNER

Photographs: George Brun, Aix-les-Bains - Giraudon, Paris - Ralph
Kleinhempel, Hamburg - Otto Nelson, New York -
Photorama, le Havre - John Webb, London

LIBRARY OF CONGRESS CATALOG CARD NUMBER: 75-206-97 ISBN: 0-517-524775

VARENNE-SAINT-HILAIRE, VIEW FROM CHAMPIGNY, 1863
Oil 19 3/4" x 28 3/4"
Museum of Fine Arts, Budapest

Before going into the details of Pissarro's life and work, it is necessary to put both of these in an appropriate frame of reference, for the part that human emotion and human behavior played in his development is extremely significant. Pissarro could almost be said to illustrate in microcosm the situation of all of the innovative artists of his era; his originality is so typical of the artists of the latter part of the nineteenth century that one is continually tempted to draw general conclusions from his individual case. He was so independent as barely to escape being anarchistic; so intransigent in his dedication to art that any other unrelated activity seemed to him a compromise; confident of the future even at moments of his greatest distress; so carefree that he could become the father of a large family at a time when his future was at best uncertain; and able in his own mind logically to reconcile all these contradictions without relinquishing any part of his great honesty and profound sense of humanity.

Two elements above all must be taken into consideration if one wishes thoroughly to understand the wellsprings of the man and his art: first, the birth date of the artist (1830) and consequently the many years (he died in 1903) during which he was able to observe and in a number of instances to participate passionately in the diverse political and artistic movements of the second half of the nineteenth century, from the aftermath of romanticism and the gaudy excesses of the Second Empire to the revolutionary victories of the New Republic.

He had the opportunity to become familiar with these struggles and to enter into them with a maturity — at least as far as the arts were concerned — which was not possible for the other founders of the Impressionist movement, for whom he was always a respected elder statesman. Monet was born in 1840; Renoir in 1841; Sisley and Cézanne in 1839. Thus they were all obout ten years younger than he. The difference in age becomes still more striking when it comes to the neo-Impressionists (Seurat was born in 1859 and Signac in 1863) with whom Pissarro was also linked, and to whom he brought the weight of his experience and authority.

The other element essential to our understanding of the man consists of his boundless enthusiasm, his good will, his insatiable curiosity about any experience which might possibly enrich the language of the painter; an alert mind, open to any suggestion which might, in his opinion, show him the way better to serve his art and to avoid getting into a rut. The enduring quality of his art stems from the continuing independence from any routine established either by himself or others; it results in changes in technique which occasionally seem to indicate a certain instability and often disconcert dealers and collectors, who like to rediscover in an artist those characteristics to which they are accustomed.

Yet it is unjust to state that Pissarro was too easily influenced, as some critics have done. The truth is that he always regarded sympathetically the innovations of others in their work, for he possessed the conscious modesty of an artisan who, observing new techniques, sought to determine which ones he could utilize to enrich and better serve his goal.

This goal — and we see in it another aspect of his constant concern — was always to portray nature as sensitively as possible, to capture its fundamental and eternal quality as well as the changes wrought by light and the seasons. For him the reality of nature lay in its close intimacy with man; hence the appeal of the gestures of peasants, of groupings of people engaged in everyday acts; his affectionate attention to the lives of the humble.

Of all the Impressionists, Pissarro is the one who has most strongly emphasized the presence of people in his landscapes. The others have almost always treated these two

6

Kneeling Woman. Drawing Louvre Museum, Paris

subjects separately and independently. At any given time, they have generally been either landscape or portrait artists, and it is rare that one or the other of these two aspects of their art does not dominate any individual work. Only Pissarro brings into harmony all the elements of a scene depicting peasants at work or women in a market place. There is total accord between the people and the settings, and it is because of this that, viewing his workers in the fields, some persons have found a certain kinship with Millet.

In both of these artists there is the same respect and sympathetic attitude toward humble everyday tasks, the same rejection of all artificiality. Yet one discovers on studying them closely that the two men have set their feet along very different paths. In the people of Millet there is a mystic, religious quality, and one is frequently tempted to read a sort of symbolism in their presentation. His peasants are prototypes, almost archetypes.

There is nothing of the sort in Pissarro's work. If he observed the truth with a fidelity equal to that of Millet, he was content merely to show his liking for commonplace things. Millet was determined to point up a moral; Pissarro, on the other hand, was dedicated to expressing eternal verities without any undercurrent of social philosophy, which does not at all mean that he was indifferent to the condition of man.

Less widely noted have been the ties which bind him to another acute observer of life, Daumier, to whom Pissarro is often more closely linked than he is to Millet, in large part through his drawing, through the nervous suppleness of his strokes and his manner of rendering expressive faces and natural attitudes. For him, as for Millet and Daumier, man is at the same time a social creature and a component of artistic production; his presence is as essential to a painting as any other natural ingredient. As a matter of fact, Pissarro did not hide his admiration for Daumier. In February 1884, from Osny, he wrote to his son Lucien: « I sent you some lithographs by Daumier... they are completely marvelous from every point of view. I find it impossible to look at them without having the highest regard for this great artist. You should pay attention to the fact that they are telling mainly because they are admirably constructed. Take the construction of the arms, the legs, the feet; it is as spectacularly successful as the drawings of the great masters... and these are caricatures! Notice the ties, the collars, the trousers, the folds which are so well drawn at the bottom; notice the shoes and the hands! »

As we have stated, Pissarro had no desire to deliver a spiritual or political message through his brush; even less, in his experimental efforts, did he seek originality for its own sake, as a hallmark of distinctiveness. Yet he was willing to be unorthodox when that suited his graphic needs, even at the risk of appearing inconsistent by abandoning those techniques which he had formerly found useful. The stages in his evolution are invariably marked by the discovery of a *modus operandi* suited to his current perceptions. Mr. Alfredo Boulton, in his penetrating analysis of Pissarro's youthful work, done in the Antilles and Venezuela, shows to what extent his drawings and paintings of the period resemble the work of his Danish friend, Fritz Melbye. Later, after arriving in France, Pissarro did not conceal his admiration for Corot; and when he became a practitioner of Impressionism, he demonstrated free and open strokes, a mastery in portraying the vibra-

Madame Pissarro sewing, 1858. Oil 6 1/4" x 4 3/8". Ashmoleum Museum, Oxford

The little factory, 1863.
Oil 10 1/2" x 15 7/8"
Museum of Modern Art, Strasbourg

10

JALLAIS HILL, PONTOISE, 1867.
Oil 34 1/4" x 45 1/4"
Metropolitan Museum of Art, New York. Gift of William Church

On the Banks of the Marne, winter 1866
Oil 36 1/4" x 59".
Art Institute, Chicago

THE STAGECOACH TO LOUVECIENNES, 1870
Oil 9 7/8" x 13 3/4"
Jeu de Paume Museum, Paris

14

BOULEVARD DES FOSSES, PONTOISE, 1872
Oil 9 7/8" x 13 3/4"
Collection Norton Simon, Los Angeles

THE FIELDS, 1868. Oil 6 3/4" x 11 7/8". Museum of Bagnols-sur-Cèze

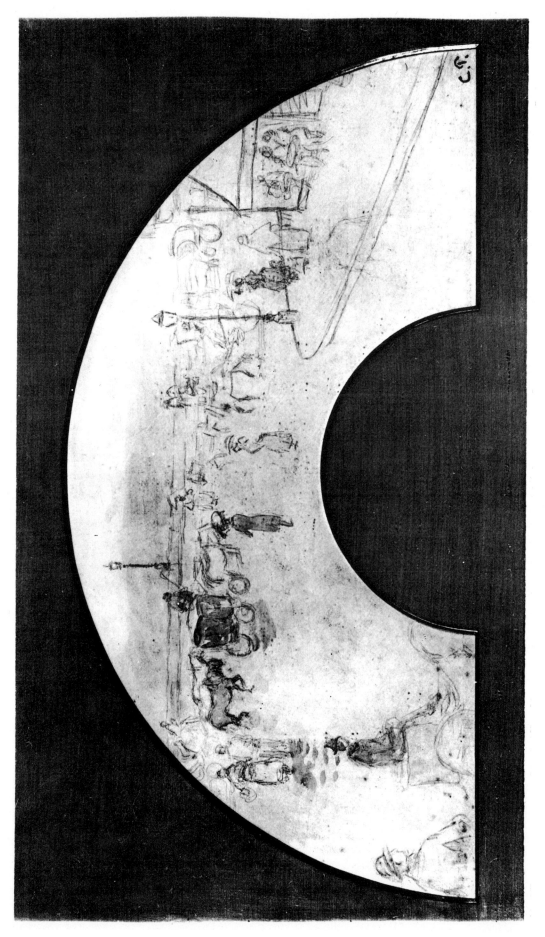

View of Paris. Water color and pencil 11 3/4" x 23 1/2". Collection Mr. and Mrs. Nathan Cummings, New York

Entry into the village of Voisins, 1872
Oil 18 1/8" x 21 5/8"
Jeu de Paume Museum, Paris

18

no 1 - 4e état   la Masure   C. Pissarro.

The Old Cottage, 1879. Etching and aquatint, 4th stage 5 5/8" x 6 3/4".
Museum of Fine Arts, Boston. Ellen Frances Mason

20

tions of light and the shimmering instability of landscapes equal to that of his most illustrious contemporaries.

In the period of neo-Impressionism, Pissarro became convinced of the virtues of a division of tones (pointillism) and created atmosphere with a more subtle luminosity. When, after several years spent submitting himself to this discipline, he gave it up, it was because he feared that the too rigid formula on which the process was based might tend to make the artist forget the essence of reality. In any case, although he might accept external support, he was never blindly submissive to its demands. He asked of it only that it supply him with the tools he needed and adapted these to his own temperament, in this way accomplishing an act which was personal to him, even though inspired by something external.

All of Pissarro's work represents an intimate union between his concept of reality and his emotions as an artist; it reflects a sincere and unaffected feeling, supported by a knowledgeable technique, which in no way reduces the impact of the initial sensation. This achievement — maintaining the freshness of a first impression — is what gives the art of Pissarro its brilliance and spontaneity; it characterizes his output from the beginning to the end of his long career, and is the explanation and justification for every step he took during his evolution as an artist.

THE FIRST STEPS

Seen from a certain angle, any life can be said to be typical of its time. This is especially true where the life of an artist is concerned, since the evolution of the life and the work which it brings into being exemplify the relationship of the man to his era, its manner of being and of thinking — that is, the basic style of the period. To speak of Pissarro is not merely to enumerate the episodes of his life or the list of his works; it is not merely to put him in his proper place in the school of Impressionism, of which he was one of the most brilliant examples. It is also to put Impressionism in its proper place in relation to all of the art of the nineteenth century; it is to point out the place of art and artists in contemporary society and to indicate the profound political turbulence which agitated the era.

The opportunity to observe the historical relevance of a single life is particularly good where Pissarro is concerned, for, as we have said, he lived through the most diversified events, was acquainted with conflicting artistic and political movements and participated in the most fiery combats during a period of history rich in passion, in experimentation and innovation.

In addition, because of his special traits, Camille Pissarro more than any other

LOWER NORWOOD, 1870
Oil 14" x 18"
National Gallery, London

22

PONTOISE, BANKS OF THE OISE, 1872
Oil 24 1/4" x 28 3/4"
Collection Norton Simon Foundation, Los Angeles

Portrait of Lucien, 1874. Lithograph in original state. 9 1/2" x 8"
Museum of Fine Arts, Boston. Stephen Bullard Memorial.

Impressionist felt driven to take part in history, to play an active role as a man with a responsibility to society. Let us recall what his life was like, both from a personal point of view and also from the perspective of his participation in a vast panorama of ideas and accomplishments.

Camille Pissarro was born on July 10,1830, on what was then a Danish island in the West Indies, in Saint Thomas, where his father had a flourishing hardware business in the port of Charlotte-Amalie. We know little about his parents, except that his father, Abraham Gabriel Pissarro, was a French Jew of Portuguese origin and that his mother, Raquel Manzano, was Creole. This mixed heritage cannot really explain any of the physical

PORTRAIT OF JEANNE HOLDING A FAN, 1873. Oil 21 5/8" x 18 1/8". Ashmoleum Museum, Oxford

features or moral characteristics of the artist; nor was Camille Pissarro influenced by the recollections of his exotic background in the same way Paul Gauguin was to be later on. Very early Camille showed an exceptional gift for drawing; this was not initially encouraged by his parents, who preferred to think his future would be that of a businessman.

In 1841, his family decided to send him to France for his studies. After a long crossing, he arrived in Paris, or more accurately in Passy, to live in a boardinghouse run by a Mr. Savary. The latter, noting the gift for drawing displayed by his young boarder, and contrary to the express wishes of the boy's parents, encouraged him to perfect his talent and to persevere in his efforts to become an artist. In spite of the specific prohibition of Camille's father, who had no intention of allowing his son to develop such unspeakably bad habits, Mr. Savary, appreciating the potentialities of the young man, let him indulge in his artistic bent during his leisurely walks and on vacations and holidays, thus not interfering with his schooling or openly opposing Pissarro Senior.

When Camille was seventeen and it was felt that his education was adequate, he was recalled to Saint Thomas to begin his apprenticeship in the marts of trade. For the next five years he tried, to the best of his ability, to work simultaneously on his art and in business. But the restraint which the latter imposed on him grew more and more difficult to endure.

About 1850 the Danish painter Fritz Melbye, sent by his country to study the situation in its distant colony, noticed the youth, who was drawing in the port during the intervals in his work as a commercial employee. The two young men established friendly relations. Melbye was slightly older — he was born in 1826 — and this meant that he was slightly more advanced in his career as a painter. Camille Pissarro was deeply touched by his attention and understanding, to the point where, having listened first to the encouraging remarks and then to the proposals of the tempter, he decided to escape from business and to accompany Fritz Melbye to Caracas, Venezuela, where his newfound companion was scheduled to go to complete his government assignment.

Later, Camille Pissarro himself would spell out the reasons for this decision, which marked the starting point of his career, was the act of defiance which caused his whole future to hang in the balance. « I was living in Saint Thomas in 1852, working at a well paid business job. I felt unable to stand the situation for too much longer and, without giving my decision a second thought, I left behind everything I possessed and fled to Caracas, thus breaking the chains which bound me to a bourgeois existence ».

On November 12, 1852, the two young men arrived in the port of La Guairá and remained there for some time before going onto Caracas. Almost at once Camille Pissarro was welcomed into a milieu of extremely cultivated persons, most of them music lovers.

In August 1854 he returned to Saint Thomas alone, then in 1855 went to France to settle there permanently. Faced with overwhelmingly strong evidence of his son's artistic leanings, his father no longer tried to suppress them; he was undoubtedly also motivated by the fact that by then Camille was twenty-five years old and had displayed absolutely no talent for business, so that it seemed expedient to try to help him in a new career in which

Grandmother (Light Effect), 1889. Engraving and aquatint, 7th stage. 6 7/8" x 10 1/4". Museum of Fine Arts, Boston. Horatio S. Curtis.

BOUQUET OF PINK PEONIES, 1873. Oil 28 3/4" x 23 5/8". Ashmoleum Museum, Oxford.

he appeared to have an excellent chance of succeeding. With the consent of his family and even some modest financial support, Camille therefore set out to study his profession in Paris. No longer dependent on chance encounters or the haphazard opportunities provided by the countries he chanced to be visiting, Pissarro could now rely on association with his elders, even such masters as Camille Corot, for whom he immediately developed great admiration and who received Pissarro at his home, 58 rue Paradis-Poissonière (Fishwife's Paradise).

When he arrived in Paris, firmly resolved to devote himself to his painting, Pissarro had already evinced a certain mastery of and a clearly defined preference for landscapes. Logically, these were for the most part exotic landscapes; for several years he would recall the tropics so vividly that he would continue to depict them in all of their aspects: the vegetation demonstrated by tall palm trees, the warm coloring and also the wide horizons in the far distance, which one would find echoed and repeated later in the best of the Impressionist canvases.

Yet, in spite of the lure of his memories, he quickly became accustomed to the landscapes of France and responsive to their appeal. One factor which brought this about was the admiration he felt for the art of Corot, which we have already mentioned, with its skillful blend of artistic subtlety and polished elegance. Above all, Pissarro listened to the advice of the painter Anton Melbye, the brother of Fritz who had been his friend and counselor in the West Indies. Anton, also a painter, had been living in France since 1847 and had already earned somewhat of a reputation for himself. He received Pissarro with open arms and was so impressed by his talent that he entrusted to him the task of « finishing his skies », as Tabarant informs us in writing on the subject.

It is reasonable to think that, beginning at this time, the young man became sensitive to the social climate in which he lived and that his juvenile enthusiasm caused him to be fired by the same ardent impulses which animated the society of the period. It was in 1855 that the first large international exhibition was held early in Paris, the year when several foreign monarchs visited the French capital, among them the King of Sardinia and Queen Victoria of England. It was also the period when, early in the reign of Prince Napoleon, the direction that the world was taking — the hopes it inspired, the anxieties, the injustices, the poverty which was gradually increasing began to become apparent. It was a period of abundance, but also of assassination attempts. (There were two of them against Napoleon in the course of the year 1885.)

This effervescent atmosphere did not divert the young artist from the pursuit of his vocation. He attended different courses more or less regularly, some in private academies and some, according to report, in the École des Beaux-Arts. He worked assiduously in the academic field, but did not lose his predilection for nature and continued to put his trust in first hand observation. We must remember that he considered the advice of Corot priceless; it was compatible with a movement which, for over a decade, had tended to regard the study of landscapes as desirable and had made this subject a matter of major importance. The profound impression made by the exhibition of English landscapists in 1824, particularly Constable, had continued to increase ist impact, and the so-called schools of Fontainebleau and Barbizon, which to a certain extent had justified their existence by the observation of nature, won their titles of nobility and accumulated an ever more numerous body of supporters.

The year 1855 also offered the young man a golden opportunity to start his career and to make a ledger sheet for himself, for the fine arts section of the international exposition which had just opened included all the most famous names and opened the door to all sorts of confrontations. One such pitted Ingres against Delacroix, who were represented respectively by forty-three and thirty-five paintings. It appears that it was on the occasion of this exposition that Pissarro was seized by enthusiasm for Corot. Perhaps it was there also that he perceived a certain affinity for Daubigny and Millet. In the face of these examples, he understood that he could no longer be content to paint exotic landscapes, relying on his memories, and that first hand observation could bestow on him new bounties. At that time the countryside was at the gates of Paris and offered him easily available subject matter, permitting him to follow the advice given him by Corot: « You must go to the fields, the Muse is in the woods ». In the course of his explorations, he met another painter Ludovic Piette, slightly older then he, who was to become his bosom friend and on several occasions in the future would come to his aid. He also became acquainted with another artist, Chintreuil, who likewise was very interested in the effects of light on the landscape, as well as Jean-Alfred Desbrosses.

Still more important was his meeting in 1857 with a man ten years younger than he, whose acquaintance he made while attending the Swiss Academy: Claude Monet, who was only seventeen, not yet discharged from his military service, and who already had found himself in conflict with a bourgeois family who did not look with favor on the prospect of him embarking on the uncertain career of a painter. It is possible that the similarity between the social and family situations of the two men may have played a role in their budding friendship. In any case, their congeniality of tastes and temperaments inevitably led to a close relationship between the two and resulted in their participation in the same struggles.

The year 1859 can be considered the date of Pissarro's official debut, since for the first time he exhibited a picture at the Salon: *Landscape at Montmorency*. This first success had no tomorrow, and his submissions of 1861 and 1863 were rejected. Thus, although he had not planned it, he became a member of the group of nonconformists and in 1863 showed his colors by sending three canvases to the famous « Salon des Refusés » sponsored by Napoleon III, who proved more liberal than the opponents of the artists who, ten years later, would form the core and kernel of Impressionism. Pissarro reappeared in the subsequent Salons in 1865, 1866 and 1868 and even received some favorable comments in the press; among these was the review of Castagnary and also, a little later, one by Émile Zola.

At this point his art was evolving rapidly. From 1866 on, we see him veering away more and more from the influence of Corot. His palette grew clearer; neutral tone became

Self-Portrait, about 1890. Etching, 3rd stage. 7 3/8" x 7".
Museum of Fine Arts, Boston. Lee M. Friedman.

rarer and rarer; air began to circulate more lightly in a luminous space. Those traits which were characteristic of Impressionist techniques became more clearly defined; he began to paint with a palette knife, with sweeping and ever more supple strokes.

In order to be closer to his sources of inspiration, he established residence in the suburbs of Paris. His landscapes, set in Montmorency, La Varenne, Pontoise and, beginning in 1869, in Louveciennes, date his domiciles; the Paris addresses which appear after his name in the catalogue of the Salon are those of his agents or buyers. For example, one is the address of Father Martin, a former singer turned secondhand dealer who bought from Pissarro part of his output, paying twenty, thirty or forty francs a canvas, according to the size, and thus assuring the artist of an income which was certainly modest but a less

View of Rouen, Bon Secours Road, 1883.
Drawing Collection, Louvre Museum, Paris.

HARVEST IN MONTEFOUCAULT, 1876
Oil 25 5/8" x 36 1/4"
Jeu de Paume Museum Paris

33

RESTING IN THE WOODS, PONTOISE, 1878. Oil 25 5/8" x 21 1/4". Kunsthalle Hamburg.

34

PATH IN THE WOODS IN SUMMER, 1877. Oil 31 7/8" x 25 5/8". Jeu de Paume Museum, Paris.

KITCHEN GARDEN AND TREE IN BLOSSOM, SPRING, 1877
Oil 25 5/8" x 31 7/8"
Jeu de Paume Museum, Paris

CHAPONVAL LANDSCAPE, 1880
Oil 21 1/4" x 25 5/8"
Jeu de Paume Museum, Paris

PEASANT WOMAN, 1880
Oil 28 3/4" x 23 5/8". National Gallery of Art, Washington D.C. Chester Dale

38

POULTRY MARKET IN PONTOISE, 1882
Oil 45 1/2" x 31 3/4". Collection Norton Simon, Los Angeles

STILL LIFE AND FLOWERS IN VASE, 1878
Oil 32" x 25 1/2". Collection Mr. and Mrs. Nathan Cummings, New York

chancy operation than waiting for a potential client who might never materialize.

When he came to Paris, he was a regular customer of the Guerbois café, avenue de Clichy, which since the winter of 1867-1868 had become a gathering place for novelists, critics and painters, a spot where they could meet and exchange ideas. There he saw Manet, Renoir, Degas, Fantin-Latour, Bracquemond, and writers such as Duranty, Armand Sylvestre, Zacharie Astruc and even, on occasion, Zola.

Until 1870 he stayed in Louveciennes, to which he had moved in 1868. Then, faced with the threat of an invasion by the German army, he decided to decamp to Montfoucault, in the department of the Mayenne, where he was received by his friend Ludovic Piette. Shortly thereafter he set sail for England.

Without his realizing it, one cycle had been completed. All of the years up until then can be considered a period of apprenticiship. What he accomplished from that time on would be the result of a definite commitment, which would be reaffirmed from year to year as the effects multiplied. The sojourn in London would be not only a time of exile and anxiety while Pissarro awaited the day of his return to France, but would mark a breach with the past as well as a new departure. As a matter of fact, at that very moment some events were taking place which would have a decisive influence on the future of Impressionism. Pissarro regularly visited Monet, who had also taken refuge in England, and as a result of their exchange of ideas, the details of the new art were developed, and it became freer. They went to museums together and discovered Turner, his luminous palette, the transparency of his material, his fairy like vision of nature, his way of painting clouds without freezing them in place.

It was also in London that Daubigny, like them a refugee, introduced them to a French art dealer who likewise was waiting for better days, Paul Durand-Ruel. The latter, interested in the imaginative and innovative art of the young men, bought several paintings from them. Pissarro was very grateful for these purchases, for he had even less success in London than in Paris. A letter to his friend Theodore Duret, which remained unpublished until Tabarant reproduced it, summarized the situation very well. « I will not remain here; it is only when one is in a foreign country that one realizes how beautiful, vast and hospitable France is. What a difference here! I receive only scorn, indifference and even coarse abuse; my colleagues display the most selfish kind of jealousy and distrust. Here there is no such thing as art; everything is business. Yet as far as business and selling go, I have gotten nowhere, except for Durand-Ruel who bought two small pictures from me. My painting is not catching on, not at all; that becomes obvious wherever I go ».

As soon as possible, therefore, Pissarro returned to France. He did not find a single one of the fifteen hundred paintings which he had left in his studio in Louveciennes; and apparently this loss served as another road sign pointing to a new departure. He had already reached his fortieth birthday, and yet he had retained sufficient boldness and freedom of spirit to follow a new direction and blaze a new trail. He began over again, liberated from his past; henceforth he would possess a more assured technique and a clearer vision of what he wanted to accomplish: that is, to question nature.

ROUEN, BURIAL OF CARDINAL BONNECHOSE, 1883
Watercolor 8 11/16" x 11 7/16"

42

THE PRICE OF LIBERTY
1871-1880

Once again Pissarro took up residence in Pontoise, in the quarter of the Hermitage which had previously been the inspiration for several fine pictures in 1868-1869. He found in the vicinity the same familiar landscapes, as well as those of Osny and Auvers, where Cézanne went at that same period to find subjects for some important canvases. There is every reason to think that the two artists influenced one another: Cézanne showing Pissarro the way to simplify his compositions and to structure them more solidly; Pissarro giving Cézanne the example of more luminous painting composed of lighter matter. Thanks to them, and simultaneously to the other artists who had remained in Paris, Impressionism was in the process of evolving; the artists became close to one another as a result of their mutuality of interests and their new found friendship, without being aware that they were paving the way for a veritable revolution.

For some time, in spite of enormous financial difficulties, the stars appeared favorable. With some reason, they had high hopes. At the beginning of the year 1874, in a sale at the Hôtel Drouot, seven canvases of Pissarro brought very respectable prices in the two-hundred to three-hundred-and-fifty-franc range. One of them was even auctioned off for a sum which in the artist's eyes was utterly fabulous: nine hundred and fifty francs.

At the Swiss Academy where, in 1857, he had made the acquaintance of Monet, he met Cézanne and Guillaumin several years later. His friendship with Renoir and Sisley appears to have begun about 1865. Therefore at this juncture the young artists had known each other for almost ten years, and in some cases slightly longer. These years of their association and continuing exchange of ideas had persuaded each one of them that the sympathetic relationships they had established were far from superficial and were based on a genuine community of interests. The benevolence of Pissarro, as well as the fact that he was the oldest member of the group, gave him a certain authority in the eyes of his young friends, and he was frequently able to serve as an arbiter and to settle the slight misunderstandings which inevitably arise between men of impulsive temperament. Although they were not aware of it, the time of maturity and struggle had come. The year 1874 was decisive; it would become the date of a collective crisis of conscience imposed by circumstances; not willed by them, but accepted courageously.

A milestone would be the exhibition they decided to organize, together with some other painters who, like them, were dissatisfied with the rigidity of the jury of the Salon and reluctant to make any further efforts to renew relationships with the academicians. The group took as its name the somewhat banal: « Association of Painters, Sculptors and Engravers », and that in itself should be sufficient to prove that at that moment they had no intention of raising any hackles. On April 15, this dissident Salon opened its doors in quarters on the boulevard des Capucines, kindly lent them by the photographer Nadar.

Immediately, contrary to expectations, it created a sensation. The press, which was annoyed, and the public, which was hilarious, both indulged in cutting sarcasm, and their lack of understanding finally gave rise to anger. Never had an exhibition of paintings inspired such loud cries of outrage. A few years earlier Manet, with his *Lunch on the Grass* and *Olympia*, had been accused of threatening public morality; this time no one could attack the subject matter since, for the most part, it consisted of landscapes. Therefore it was the painting itself, the unfamiliar technique, which caused an explosion of adverse criticism.

How to explain the paintings' provocative quality, which was so strong that the public objected violently in spite of the innocuousness of the subjects? The key may lie in the canvas of Claude Monet: *Impression, Rising Sun,* which was hung in the exhibition, and which was a prime source of indignation. The author of an article in the paper « The Charivari » used this picture to demonstrate the ridiculousness of the new art form and invented the term « Impressionists » to describe the pseudo-innovators.

The word immediately caught on and was soon adopted by the very artists it had been invented to ridicule. It accurately spelled out the reason for the shock effect: How could one presume to paint anything as insubstantial as an impression? Up until then painting had always depicted something real: a person, a place, an object, a thing which could be seen and then reproduced. But an impression! That was a joke and gave license to do anything at all; least so it seemed to those who surveyed the handiwork of the young rebels.

In truth, the Impressionists little by little were perfecting a technique which enabled them to suggest the impressions produced by the spectacle of life and most especially the elements which made up a landscape: the sparkle of water, the quivering of leaves, the vibrations of light. During the years that followed they persisted in their efforts to improve this technique, nor did they allow themselves to be distracted by scorn or the failure to sell their canvases.

Although amazed by a torrent of abuse which they had not foreseen, they did not become discouraged and, once the surprise was over, decided to enter the lists and battle public hostility. Their first act threw down the gauge: the excitement caused by the exhibition had barely died down when they announced a public auction. It took place on March 24, 1875, arousing a new burst of indignation. Nevertheless, it achieved some measure of success, since the seventy pictures offered for sale brought a total of ten thousand three hundred and forty-nine francs, that is to say an average of almost a hundred and fifty francs a picture, which, in view of the circumstances, was considerably better than might have been expected.

The following year, 1876, they organized a second exhibition, which demanded a stricter discipline of the exhibitors; only those who acknowledged the infamous label of Impressionist and had made a definite commitment were accepted. The exhibition was held in the gallery of Durand-Ruel, who became recognized as a champion of the new movement, on the rue Le Peletier. On display were only nineteen paintings instead of the thirty of the preceding show, in which the artists had been united in a spirit of discontent rather than through a community of esthetic goals. The same opponents as before mobilized their

PORTRAIT OF FELIX, 1883. Oil 21 1/4" x 18 1/8". Tate Gallery, London

ROAD GOING UP TO OSNY, 1883. Oil 21 5/8" x 18 1/8". Museum of Fine Arts, Valenciennes

46

Making pea trellises, 1887. Oil. Faure Museum, Aix-les-Bains

Apple trees in blossom, 1885-1890
Oil 5 7/8" x 9".
Faure Museum, Aix-les-Bains

48

forces, but now the allies were more numerous and outspoken and so encouraged the artists that they got ready for a third exhibition.

This took place in April 1877 at 6 rue Le Peletier, and this time there were eighteen exhibitors, including all of those who today are considered masters of Impressionism. Each sent an impressive number of entries: Monet, thirty pictures; Sisley, seventeen; Degas, Renoir and Pissarro, twenty-two apiece; Berthe Morisot, nineteen; Cézanne, sixteen. On the occasion of the public auction which took place several weeks later, on May 28, the prices paid for Pissarro's work were modest, ranging from fifty to two hundred and sixty francs. During that same period, Durand-Ruel was suffering financial reverses and was unable to subsidize the artists as generously as he would have liked.

The fourth exhibition, in 1879 at 28 avenue of the Opéra, had some notable absentees — Renoir, Sisley and Cézanne — but was graced for the first time by the presence of Gauguin, modestly represented by a single sculpture.

The fifth exhibition in 1880, at 10 rue des Pyramides, had the same absentees plus Monet, but this time Gauguin had several paintings on display.

The sixth and seventh exhibitions were held in 1881 and 1882. They were the last ones prior to the eighth and final showing, which did not take place until 1886. The group dispersed after a series of disagreements whose roots were both emotional and esthetic and which resulted from the strongly individualistic personalities of the members; from the fact that their new found success put some of them higher on the ladder of fame than others; and from the tumultuous political atmosphere of the period, in which some of them became fanatic partisans of one side or the other. Whatever trials and tribulations the future might bring, the most difficult times and the days of gnawing poverty were almost over for the majority of the men who, in 1874, had sounded the call to battle.

At each successive exhibition the number of connoisseurs increased, but not the number of collectors. As early as the fourth exhibition, in 1879, enough visitors had been attracted to the show to give each artist who participated a net profit of four hundred and thirty-nine francs. Yet sales increased slowly thereafter.

Because the exhibitions followed one another at more or less regular intervals, they pointed up the diversity of the artists' styles. One or the other was accused of being a nonconformist when he adopted an individual technique of his own or welcomed to the group new supporters (Gauguin, Seurat, Signac) who did not have the unanimous approval of the older members. These newcomers did not really rejuvenate the group; on the other hand, they sharpened the disagreements. Nevertheless, despite the clash of styles and personalities, certain traits remained characteristic of the group as a whole, and in no one did they shine more brilliantly than in Pissarro. Heading the list was the luminous atmosphere which bathed all the landscapes, and which was obtained by using pure colors and refusing to use black. There was also the sensation of pulsating life, achieved by the juxtaposition of tiny brushstrokes. And above all there was a radiant flowering, a fidelity to nature which rejected all artificiality and narrative lines and made a picture an end in itself rather than the servant of a storyteller or a moralist.

The Haymaker,
1890.
Etching,
12th stage.
7 3/4" x 5 1/4".
National Library,
Print Collection,
Paris

50

Study for
« The Cat. »
Charcoal.
Drawing
Collection,
Louvre Museum, Paris

The world as seen by Pissarro is a wise world, a little austere without being overly harsh; a world in good moral and physical health, which shows no trace of the desperate misery experienced by the artist. Gradually he gained the backing of a small group of collectors and this enabled him to survive, albeit precariously, in view of his responsibilities as the father of a large family. For Pissarro had seven children, born between 1863 and 1884, and the burden was an onerous one. He spent a great deal of his time going from one client to another trying to raise a few vitally needed francs.

« Does Mama », he wrote to his son Lucien, « think business is so good? Does she really believe that I find it fun to run around in the snow and the mud from morning till night without a sou in my pockets, begrudging the pennies it costs to take a coach when I am dog tired, hesitating before investing in a meager lunch or dinner? I can tell you it is no picnic. But I ask only one thing: to find a man with enough confidence in my talent to provide me and my family with the money needed to live on. I am happy only when I am in Eragny with all of you, tranquilly dreaming of my next picture. Lord am I asking too much »?

Yet one can never find the slightest hint of discouragement in Pissarro's paintings. His art is serious without being sad; it reflects a serene equanimity, as if nothing mattered to him but the art of painting. His landscapes belong to an untroubled world; the artist, who observed this world, was preoccupied only with depicting what he saw. Even in his letters, he was more apt to dwell on what concerned his art than on the vicissitudes of his daily life. And when the burden became too heavy and he did touch on his troubles, he merely expressed his anxiety and worry in a few words and then returned at once to the problems he had as an artist.

In everything he did Pissarro demonstrated a benevolence and a desire to be understood which rendered him vastly sympathetic. The only times he was guilty of making any adverse criticisms were when he questioned the motivations of his comrades; thus he was slightly disheartened when Gauguin seemed to him to have an overly practical business sense or when Manet appeared intransigent and even biased in the fact of the attempts of Renoir and Monet to be accepted by the Salon. But these reservations were superficial and were soon replaced by more friendly assessments.

In a few lines, Tabarant limned a living portrait of the man:

« Pissarro, he said, was always happy to praise his comrades. He engaged in gently barbed irony and occasionally had a sharp tongue, yet never did a really pejorative word pass his lips or flow from his pen. Every time that what he called the camp of his friends was threatened by a schism, he jumped in to mediate, and the quarrels were immediately resolved, thanks of his good humor and lighthearted teasing, which the cruelty of his struggle for existence never managed to suppress ».

Gradually the colleagues of the early years were augmented by other supporters, esthetes and writers, some of whom he met at the café of the New Athens: Theodore Duret, Castagnary, Émile Zola, Duranty, Hoschede, the pastry king Eugene Murer, and also tradesmen, dealers and entrepreneurs such as Tanguy and Portier.

TREES IN BAZINCOURT, 1887
Aquarelle 6 7/8" x 10"

53

C. Pissarron

Peasant Woman at the Well, study about 1891. Etching in original state. 12 1/2" x 8 7/8".
Library of the Institute of Art and Archeology, Paris

THE PARTING OF THE WAYS
1880-1890

The years 1880-1885 were particularly important for all of the group and brought about numerous changes in their lives and works.

In 1881 Renoir, after a first trip to Italy, came back deeply impressed by Raphael; so much so that he initiated a new style of painting, with smoother surfaces and more clearly defined forms. Subsequently, beginning in 1884, he branched out into an entirely new path which, in his judgment, led him definitely away from Impressionism.

In 1883 Monet settled in Giverny and from then on drew on it for most of his subject matter.

In 1884 Pissarro established residence at Eragny-sur-Epte, which until the end of his life would be the gathering place of the Pissarro family.

In 1882, a particularly acute financial crisis was felt in the business world, once again undermining the solvency of Durand-Ruel and forcing Gauguin to give up his career as a banker.

The absence of Cézanne, Renoir, Sisley and Monet from the exhibition of 1881, which we have previously noted, heralded the forthcoming dissolution of the group.

In 1885 Seurat worked out the final details of his pointillism technique, worked on the execution of *La Grande Jatte* and made the acquaintance of Pissarro.

Beginning in 1878 Cézanne, who had gone back to Provence to work, stayed there for longer and longer periods and soon was revisiting Paris only infrequently.

Several of the artists in the group tried once more to overcome the hostility of the jury of the official Salon and occasionally succeeded: apparent evidence that they had made a truce with tradition and had renounced their revolutionary tenets. Yet, discouraged by the unsatisfactory results of this orthodoxy, one after another they all ceased trying to obtain the official seal of approval. At the same time Durand-Ruel was starting to plan one-man shows for each one of them. Pissarro's took place in May 1883.

That same year, Gauguin spent several days with Pissarro in Osny, near Pontoise, and side by side they painted the same landscapes. Then Pissarro went to Rouen, where Gauguin soon came to live with his family. After having been at a very low ebb, the business of Durand-Ruel was beginning to expand and prosper; this was especially true of the overseas market, in particular London and even more the United States.

To all of these changes which affected Pissarro, there would soon be added a new pictorial experiment. The one essential ingredient of his character, which explains the various stages in his evolution and his seeming inconsistencies, is his instinctive drive for independence, an intuitive nonconformism which made him commit himself wholly to the causes he thought good, both in the realm of art and in the field of politics. By a curious paradox, this love of liberty and of novelty led him to aid and abet whatever appeared to be original, to become an ardent and courageous advocate of innovators and to back

YOUNG FLEMISH MAID, 1896. Oil 21 7/16" x 17 3/3". Stephen Hahn Gallery, New York

PEASANT WOMAN WITH BASKET, about 1889. Oil 6 1/4" x 7". Faure Museum, Aix-les-Bains

WOMAN IN AN ENCLOSURE. SPRING SUNSHINE IN AN ERAGNY FIELD, 1887
Oil 21 1/4" x 25 5/8"
Jeu de Paume Museum, Paris

58

BOUNTIFUL HARVEST, 1893
Oil 18 1/4" x 21 3/4"
Collection Mr. and Mrs. Nathan Cummings, New York

CHURCH IN KNOCKE, 1894
Oil, 21 1/4" x 25 5/8"
Jeu de Paume Museum, Paris

them to the hilt, sometimes at the risk of having to submit to a strict discipline in the name of the right to independence. The natural attraction he felt for the young, his need to take part in ideological conflicts and his generosity of spirit explain his successive support of various movements and his involvement with groups of men younger than himself, in whom he found the fresh enthusiasm of neophytes and the sort of wholehearted commitment of which he too was capable, in defiance of the passage of years and disillusionment.

He was an elder statesman of the Impressionists, but shared with them a zest for combat. Yet when, after several years spent trying to advance the movement, they appeared on the point of succeeding, he did not hesitate to give up the benefits which might accrue and engage instead in a new perilous enterprise, the pointillist movement of Seurat and his disciples, for whom he was one again a respected elder and indeed a patriarch.

Then, after a period of experimentation, he became convinced that this technique, too, was unproductive as far as he was concerned, and was bold enough to abandon it and become a solitary crusader once more; more solitary then ever, since his supporters were somewhat disaffected by his winding progress along a trail which appeared to them to lead nowhere; more solitary also because his Impressionist friends of the early days had all gone their separate ways and he had fewer resources than their stellar members.

As a matter of fact, Pissarro was the one who remained the most faithful to the Impressionist credo and who perceived the most clearly its aims and the means to achieve them. John Rewald, in his *History of Impressionism*, quotes some typical advice which Pissarro gave a young painter, Louis Le Bail:

« An artist », he said, « must seek that aspect of nature which is compatible with his temperament and choose his subject matter more for its form and color than for its design possibilities. It is futile to outline and thereby restrict forms, nor is it necessary. Precise drawing is sterile and detracts from the effect of the ensemble; it lessens the impact of sensation. Do not freeze the contours of things; it is the proper function of color, of light and shade, to produce a design. What is most difficult in dealing with a mass in painting is not to begin with the outlines but to paint what is inside. You should paint the essence of things, seek to express it by whatever means are available without regard to the details of craftsmanship. In painting you should choose a subject, notice what is to the right and what to the left, and work on everything simultaneously. Do not do it piece by piece; paint the whole by putting hues all over the canvas and stressing the color and depth by your brush strokes, while observing what lies alongside. You should work with little strokes and put down immediately what you perceive. The eye should not concentrate on a particular spot but should see everything and, at the same time, observe the reflections of the colors on surrounding objects. You should work simultaneously on sky, water, trees and earth, go forward boldly and constantly come back to make adjustments until you have what you want. Cover the canvas after the first session; then proceed to improve it until you can find nothing more to do. Observe carefully the aerial perspective, from the foreground to the horizon, the reflection of the sky, the leaves. Do not be afraid to use color; refine the painting little by little. Do not proceed according to a set of

« *The Struggle-for-Lifers* », 1890. *Unpublished drawing excerpted from* « *Social Depravity* » *published in facsimile by Albert Skira Art Publications, Geneva, 1972*

« Suicide of an Abandoned Woman », 1890. *Unpublished drawing excerpted from « Social Depravity »*
published in facsimile by Albert Skira Art Publications, Geneva, 1972

Bather with Geese, 1895. Etching, 10th stage. 5" x 6 7/8"
British Museum, London

dogmatic rules, but paint what you see and what you feel. Paint freely and without hesitation, for it is important to set down the first impression. Do not be timid when you face nature; be daring, at the risk of making mistakes or being deceived. You should have but one master: nature; it is she you must always consult ».

His later advocacy of the theories of the neo-Impressionists is not a disavowal made impulsively or based on a frivolous infatuation, rather it is a lucid position taken after much reflection in the hope it might enable him to build on his previous experiences and enhance his artistic potential. He made the acquaintance of Seurat in 1885 through Signac and at once evinced an interest in the new theories, which proposed to strengthen Impressionism by giving it a solid base and making use of the knowledge which had been acquired on composition and the division of colors.

THE BATHER, 1895. Oil 13 3/4" x 10 5/8".
National Gallery of Art, Washington D.C. Chester Dale

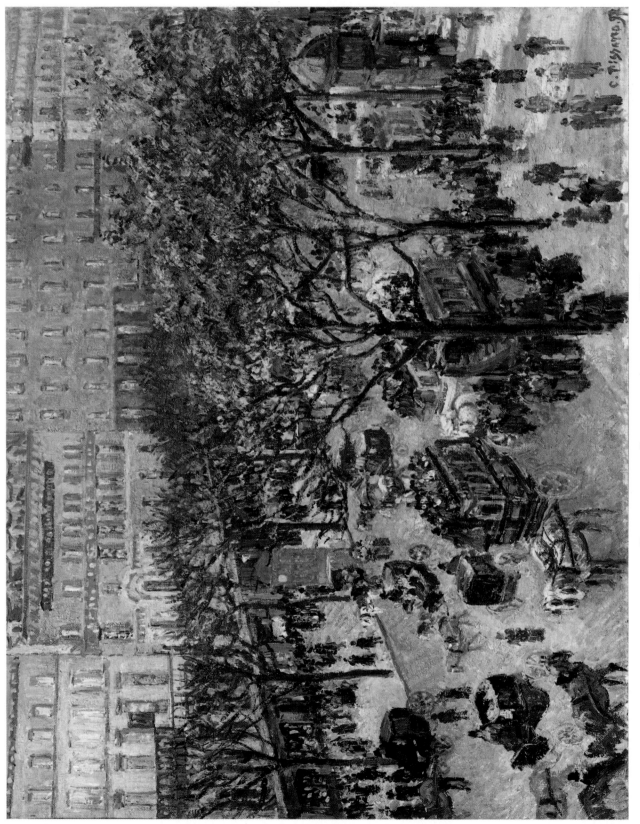

BOULEVARD DES ITALIENS, MORNING SUN, 1897
Oil 28 3/4" x 36 1/4". National Gallery of Art, Washington, D.C. Chester Dale

SQUARE OF THE THÉÂTRE FRANÇAIS, AFTERNOON WINTER SUN, 1900
Oil 29 1/8" x 36 5/8". Collection Norton Simon, Los Angeles

THE PONT-NEUF, 1902. Oil, 2nd series, 21 5/8" x 18 1/8". Museum of Fine Art, Budapest

68

The initial inspiration of the founders of Impressionism could thus, in his opinion, be fortified by a solid structure with the power to transform what had been revolutionary art into a new form of classicism with roots in scientific principles. In 1884 Seurat, executing *The Bath,* had not yet quite perfected his method. But, beginning in 1885, he applied it in his large composition, *Sunday on the Grande Jatte,* which would be exhibited the following year in the Salon of the Independents.

From that moment on, Pissarro was convinced that the division of color into small juxtaposed patches gave a greater luminosity to the colored surface than had formerly been possible.

« I am persuaded », he wrote, « of the progress to be achieved in this genre, which can produce, at certain moments, extraordinary results ». Moreover, at the eighth Impressionist exhibition in 1886, all of the important paintings shown were executed — in little dots.

Thus Pissarro subscribed totally to those theories which led to what can be called scientific Impressionism, in contrast to the other school which he called romantic Impressionism. His sponsorship bears witness in a moving way to the enthusiasm and sincerity of this artist who, in spite of his age (he was then fifty-five), did not fear to commit himself to follow a new path. Similarly, a few years later, about 1890, he was not afraid of leaving that route when he was convinced that, for him, the possibilities in that direction were limited. Yet he did not change his course without reflection and some misgivings; for months he weighed the pros and cons of the change, and showed such a strong desire to be impartial that it could actually be interpreted as a kind of instability and irresolution. He explained the situation in several letters to his son Lucien. On September 6, 1888, he wrote:

« I think a great deal about painting without using dots (pointillism). I hope to succeed, but I haven't yet been able to solve the problem of achieving a pure tone without any harshness — to determine what can be done to retain the qualities of purity and simplicity of the pointillists and yet not lose the breadth, suppleness, freedom, spontaneity and freshness of expression of the Impressionists. This is the crux of my difficulty, and it preoccupies me. For the dot is thin, without consistency, transparent, monotonous rather than simple, even as used by Seurat, especially as used by Seurat ... ». And a little later, on February 20, 1889:

« At this time I am looking for a way to replace the use of dots; up until now I have not found the technique I seek. The execution of my work is not rapid enough, in my opinion, and there is not the instantaneous reaction of the senses which I deem essential ».

Haymaking in Eragny, 1901
Oil 21 1/4" x 25 1/2"
National Gallery of Canada, Ottawa

▷

Forest scene with two figures, 1901
Oil 21 7/16" x 18 1/2"
Collection Mr. and Mrs. Shouky A. Shaheen, Atlanta, Georgia

THE LAST YEARS
1891-1903

From 1890 on, even though there were still some difficult times ahead, things became progressively better for Pissarro. His former supporters renewed their allegiance when he forswore doctrinaire pointillism, but that does not mean that his change of heart was dictated by expediency. As we have seen, he thought over his decision at length and rejected the technique only after he concluded it was impossible to overcome a certain rigidity which he found in it. Already, at the time of the auction of May 1890, two landscapes brought the gratifying prices of twenty one hundred and fourteen hundred francs, an indication that the public was starting to consider Pissarro one of the masters of Impressionism.

His naturalness was too spontaneous to be contained for long within the confines of strictly scientific principles, and it was his impulsive nature rather than his reason which led him to become enthusiastic about a formula whose novelty seemed to him to be most promising. This same spontaneity later led him to reject the formula and opt once again for artistic freedom. As a matter of fact, the period was rife with contradictions of this sort, and the political and social life of the times gave rise to numerous misunderstandings. Under the label of democracy, government officials were guilty of the most scandalous abuses of power, and very prominent citizens became involved in the corruption. On the pretext that they were fighting for liberty, anarchists infiltrated the ranks of intellectuals and provoked them into supporting the most violent acts, including bombings and assassination of President Carnot; thus were noble and generous souls duped into defending and upholding criminality.

After Durand-Ruel's reservations during Pissarro's pointillist period, he gradually became once again an approving, albeit still occasionally hesitant, patron, and attempted to obtain higher prices for the artist's work. Toward the end of 1892, Pissarro returned from a stay in England with an important collection of canvases which keenly interested Durand-Ruel. However, his admiration did not prevent him from haggling, as Pissarro observed in his correspondence with Mirbeau.

« Durand », he wrote on November 14, « came yesterday and was pleased with everything I offered him. The Mirbeau gardens were a great hit. He took almost everything. So both of you come to look at my Kews before I ship them to Paris ».

Nevertheless, on November 22: « Nothing is yet definitely arranged with Durand-Ruel. Lord! When the artist is not thought to be indispensable, business transaction can take a long time ...The canvases have been selected and are deemed worthy of being offered to the Yankees, but there has been no final agreement on the prices, although they were supposedly set a week ago. This is not at all reassuring. Undoubtedly Durand suspects that I need funds. We are circling each other, each trying to discover a weak spot he can

Young woman mending, 1895
Oil 25 5/8" x 21 3/8". Art Institute, Chicago. Gift of Mrs. Leigh B. Block

VIEW OF BERNEVAL, 1900
Oil 28 1/2" x 35"
Collection Norton Simon, Los Angeles

▷

THE RAILROAD BRIDGE AT BEDFORD PARK, 1897
Oil 25 3/4" x 21 7/16"
Marlborough Fine Art, London

BOULEVARD MONTMARTRE, NIGHT EFFECT, 1897
Oil 21" x 25 1/2"
National Gallery, London

76

grasp. We struggle like two boxers; I am thin and out of breath, while he is thick-legged and husky. So I try to be tricky ... But that never seems to succeed ».

By November 28 the conditions had been set forth. « The Durand-Ruel affair is entering a dangerous phase ... He writes me, the sly fox, that he will agree to my prices provided that I sell only to him and charge customers three times what he pays. I answered that I ask nothing better than to triple my prices to art-loving customers, but that I do not want to tie myself down. I am waiting for his reply. If he will not go along, too bad! If I starve to death, I won't give in ».

As it happened, things turned out satisfactorily for the artist, who was obliged to make a few concessions but from then on was consistently well treated by his dealer. As a result he saw his prizes continue to rise, and his fear of poverty evaporated.

It appears probable that the Pissarro exhibition organized in 1890 by Theo Van Gogh, the brother of Vincent, at the gallery of Boussod and Valadon, with a preface to the catalogue by Gustave Geffroy, made Durand-Ruel fear the competition of other dealers. In his turn he regularly exhibited Pissarro's works thereafter and organized one-man shows for him, beginning with a very successful one in 1892 (fifty paintings and twenty-one *gouaches*) and continuing in 1893, '94, '96, '98 and 1901. Pissarro's improved financial situation enabled the artist to transform his attic in the Eragny house into a large studio and to travel extensively and thus renew his inspiration with fresh subject matter.

Eragny became the central point around which Pissarro's life revolved, the nest where the family gathered, where each one came home to collect his share of human warmth and comfort. During the periods of his greatest need, Pissarro frequently went to Paris and stayed there a few days to make the rounds of possible buyers; painful pilgrimages which really amounted to passing the hat. On this topic, the anecdote recounted by Murer, the pastry millionaire and Maecenas, is significant.

« At dessert, Renoir told us how he had run around all day, a canvas under his arm, trying to dispose of it. Everywhere they dismissed him, saying: "You are too late. Pissarro has just been here. I took his picture. A humane act; he has such a large family. Poor fellow!" This "poor fellow," repeated at every door on which he knocked, exasperated Renoir, already very unhappy that he had not sold anything. "So," he called out in the voice of an overgrown child, nervously brushing his index finger below his nose in a gesture habitual with him, "because I am a bachelor and have no children, I have to die of hunger? I am as much in the hole as Pissarro. Yet no one says of me Poor Renoir! »

Pissarro's letters are full of his anguished and exhausting fund-raising forays.

Eragny seemed a refuge, a peaceful haven where he could retreat from his everlasting monetary concerns and find tranquillity, notwithstanding the occasional grumbling of the good Mme Pissarro. The children created an affectionate atmosphere to which the parents were sensitive, and they were more inclined to be understanding than to scold. The brood quickly grew into a large family. Camille Pissarro had seven children: Lucien, born in 1863; Jeanne, in 1865; Georges, in 1871, who signed his paintings Manzana; Felix, in 1874, who chose the name of Jean Roche with which to sign his pictures; Ludovic-Rodolphe, born in 1878, known as Ludovic-Rodo; Jeanne, born in 1881; and finally Paul-Émile, born in 1884, who signed his paintings Paulémile.

It might have been expected that not a single one of them would choose an artistic career; the example of their father might well have discouraged them. But Camille, who believed in serving art uncompromisingly, was incapable of causing them to swerve from their destined paths. In a letter in which he stated: « You can imagine how anxious I am, having to leave an extremely pregnant wife alone in the country, without resources and with two children to care for... » he nevertheless remarked apropos of Guillaumin, who cherished the modest security provided by a job in the administration: « It's a hundred times better to tell the bureaucracy to go to the devil. Obviously that takes a bit of character, but one should not vacillate ».

With a father who had such ideas, how could the children not be attracted by artistic careers? All of them painted. Lucien, the oldest, sent to England at an early age, established a relationship there with some avant-garde artists, notably William Morris and his friends, and immediately adopted, joined the members of this new movement in advocating a revival of craftsmanship by artisans.

He was particularly interested in producing books in which the typography and illustrations were a compatible unit, and was especially eager to highlight wood engravings. The correspondence between him and his father contained numerous observations on this topic. He played an active role in the field, and Camille Pissarro executed for him several drawings from which he could make engravings.

Nothing could be more evocative of the family spirit at the Eragny house than the anecdote recounted by Charles Kunstler. « About 1890 Lucien, the oldest child, founded a satirical paper. Each of his brothers collaborated. Camille Pissarro contributed a drawing or a lithograph for the cover illustration. The "Guignol" was not printed. The drawings were pasted on the thick straw-colored paper which made up the pages of the periodical. A paper unique in the world, made up entirely of original works, the "Guignol" appeared one a month. At the end of the year, Lucien put the different issues together. Manzana, the second son, bound the collection either in satin or in an ornate material on which a cock was embroidered in brilliant colors. Except for the Pissarro's, no one was aware of the existence of the "Guignol." In it were caricatures of the people of the region. No one was spared, not even Pissarro Senior ».

In the course of the next few years, Pissarro made a number of trips to England, Belgium and Holland, and in his own country visited Burgundy, Rouen and Le Havre. These excursions gave him the opportunity to show the great attraction urban landscapes held for him. From behind the windows of his hotel rooms, he could look down, see and reproduce a perspective in which streets angled toward the horizon and the space above them was not cut off by high houses.

In Paris, from the Hôtel du Louvre, he could see the plaza of the Théâtre Français and the glittering length of the avenue of the Opéra; from the Hôtel de Russie, at the corner of the rue Drouot, he could follow the course of the Boulevard des Italiens; from an apartment

« Poor John », *1890. Unpublished drawing excerpted from « Social Depravity »*
published in facsimile by Albert Skira Art Publications, Geneva 1972

Rue Saint Romain in Rouen, 1896. Lithograph 7 7/16" x 5 5/8"
National Library, Print Collection, Paris

CHURCH OF SAINT JACQUES IN DIEPPE, 1901
Oil 21 1/4" x 25 5/8"
Jeu de Paume Museum, Paris

« In the Hospital », 1890. *Unpublished drawing excerpted from « Social Depravity »*
published in facsimile by Albert Skira Art Publications, Geneva, 1972

« *It is the war of the haves against the have-nots* » *1890. Unpublished drawing excerpted from*
« *Social Depravity* » *published in facsimile by Albert Skira Art Publications, Geneva 1972*

STUDY FOR
THE APPLE
PICKER,
1881-1886
Pastel,
24" x 18 1/2"

Paul-Émile Pissarro, 1895. Lithopraph in original state 3 3/4" x 4 5/8"
New York Public Library

on the rue de Rivoli, he observed the Tuileries and the Carrousel; and from the home of Mme Roland, opposite the Vert-Galant, he had a panorama of the quays, the Pont-Neuf and the Pont de la Cité.

In Le Havre, Dieppe and Rouen, he surveyed the animated activity of the ports from above. This was typical of the practices of the Impressionists, who, whatever their subject matter, did not look merely at the purely mechanical aspects of the world which surrounded them but, on the contrary, translated the rigidity of city life into the mobility of light, just as they would a field of wheat strewn with flowers and stirred by the wind.

These trips may also have been something of a red herring and have been motivated by other motives than the curiosity of an artist. In July 1894, having taken refuge in Belgium

THE PILOT'S JETTY, LE HAVRE, MORNING, GREY AND FOGGY WEATHER, 1903
Oil 25 5/8" x 31 7/8"
Tate Gallery, London.

86

MORET, THE LOING CANAL, 1902
Oil 25 5/8" x 31 7/8"
Jeu de Paume Museum, Paris

in order to avoid possible troubles with the law which might follow the assassination of President Carnot, he wrote to his son Lucien:

« I am afraid that I shall be forced to stay out of France for a while. Ever since the recent legislation enacted by the French Chamber of Deputies, it is impossible for anyone to feel secure. To think that a concierge can open your letters, that a baseless accusation can force you to flee to the frontier or molder in prison, without a chance to defend yourself! One after another my friends are leaving France. Mirbeau, Paul Adam, Bernard Lazare, Steinlen and Homont would have been arrested had they not been able to escape in time; poor Luce was captured, probably because someone denounced him. As I am on my guard against certain residents of Eragny who bear me a grudge, I will remain abroad ».

The excursions and experiences of Pissarro point up one aspect of his craftsmanship: he was sensitive to human emotion as well as on the lookout for new techniques and wished to make use of the techniques to express what was in his heart and mind. We have seen how closely he studied other artists' methods of painting; but we should not overlook the painstaking accuracy of his drawings, the delicacy of his aquarelles, the purity of his pastels. In all of these fields, he adopted a language compatible with these techniques — for example, the subject matter on the fans which were so successful.

Of all the areas of his interest, it was engraving he explored the most thoroughly and in which he obtained the best results. Better than the other painters in his group, he was able to achieve in engraving on copper, and also in lithography, the same sort of mobility and subtlety that the Impressionists brought to painting. It is true that light plays a leading role in engraving and that it was always in the foreground of Pissarro's thoughts. But in Impressionist painting light is made from the juxtaposition of colors, whereas in engraving it results from the contrasts between black and white. Pissarro uderstood this process and utilized it with a secure instinct, but also with a patiently acquired technical skill.

His first etchings date from 1863 and are few in number. About 1880, the use of aquatint permitted him greater variety, a more subtle luminosity, and he executed compositions which more and more bore witness to his mastery of his artistic tools. Up to 1879 he produced only about ten plates. As in the case of his painting, at the beginning the influence of Corot was very perceptible. Yet, by 1874, the famous portrait of Cézanne in cap and overcoat gave evidence of an enormous skill, a fully developed and very personal technique. In spite of this, when Theodore Duret, in 1878, suggested that he might sell several plates in London, he was amazed.

« I dare not believe », he wrote, « that etching attempts as tentative as mine could sell in London. I have had neither the time nor the means to devote myself to making further efforts; I need two or three more years of relentless work. The need to sell forces me to do aquarelles; for the moment I have abandoned my etching ».

Nevertheless, with a few interruptions, Pissarro continued to engrave until the eve of his death; actually, his last plate was done in 1902. He had completed a total of a hundred and twenty-seven etchings.

He did not undertake the making of lithographs until 1874 and stopped after making approximately ten plates, to return to that field only in 1894. He completed about sixty lithographic prints. In all, including drypoint engravings, etchings, aquatints and lithographs, his production in the field was close to two hundred engravings, some of which were temporarily forgotten, then rediscovered after Delteil listed a hundred and ninety-four Pissarro engravings in a catalogue.

They repeat all of the subjects treated in his pictures: countrysides with wide horizons bathed in light, city streets, port wharfs, scenes of peasant life, all portrayed with supple strokes and distinguished by the simple human atmosphere with which the artist was able to imbue his subjects.

Even though his financial situation had become much better by 1890, Pissarro was never entirely free of worries about money. Yet one has the impression that his mood and disposition were never affected by this and that it did not prevent him from moving from place to place or making frequent stays in Paris. He had just rented an apartment at 1 Morland Boulevard when he suffered an abscess in the prostate to which he succumbed on November 13, 1903.

A letter from Lucien to his father, dated September 2, 1903, seems almost to have been written to serve as an epitaph and to define the high order of art which Pissarro had produced.

« It is amazing », he observed, « how everything holds up and holds together. The first pictures, the Pontoise series, the pointillist canvases and the recent works, when seen together, form a consistent whole and do not seem to have the wide divergences which I would have expected. No matter what the influences brought to bear and the techniques used, his work consistently reveals the constant efforts to reconcile and synthesize those artistic values which are the hallmark of his art ».

RAYMOND COGNIAT

Horizontal Landscape, 1879 Etching and Aquatint, 3rd state
Museum of Fine Arts, Boston

BIOGRAPHY

1830. On July 10, Camille Pissarro was born in Saint Thomas in the Danish West Indies to Abraham Gabriel Pissarro and Raquel Manzano.

1841. He was sent to France for his schooling.

1847. He returned to Saint Thomas.

1852. He made the acquaintance of the young Danish painter Fritz Melbye, who encouraged him to continue painting and took him to Venezuela.

1854. Once more he came back to Saint Thomas.

1855. He left to stay permanently in France and to study painting there, at the School of Beaux-Arts and the Swiss Academy. This was the year he met Corot; also the year of an international exhibition in Paris.

1856-1858. He worked in the vicinity of Paris, in Montmorency and La Roche-Guyon.

1859. He exhibited at the Salon and met Monet at the Swiss Academy.

1860. He met Chintreuil.

1861. He made the acquaintance of Cézanne and Guillaumin at the Swiss Academy; painted in Montmartre.

1863. He exhibited in the « Salon des Refusés ». The first son of Camille Pissarro, Lucien, was born on February 20.

1864. He exhibited in the Salon; painted in Montfoucault and La Varenne-Saint-Hilaire.

1865. Pissarro's daughter Jeanne, known as Minette, was born. He took up residence in Pontoise and became somewhat estranged from Corot.

1867. Opening of the Suez Canal.

1868. Daubigny was instrumental in getting two views of Pontoise by Pissarro hung in the Salon. Pissarro did some business with Guillaumin. Zola mentioned Pissarro in the articles he wrote on the Salon.

1869. Pissarro moved to Louveciennes. One of his pictures was shown in the Salon, and he met other artists at the Guerbois café.

1870. Fleeing the German invasion, Pissarro took refuge with his friend Ludovic Piette in Montfoucault, in Brittany, then set sail for England. In London he was reunited with Claude Monet and Paul Durand-Ruel. He married Julie Vellay.

1871. He returned to France and found that the paintings he had left in Louveciennes had all been distroyed. On November 22 his son Georges, later known as Manzana Pissarro, was born.

1872. He went back to Pontoise and found Cézanne and Guillaumin there.

1873. Pissarro worked in Pontoise, Osny, and Auvers-sur-Oise. There was a severe financial crisis. It would take Pissarro several years to straighten out his affairs.

1874. In January, at a public auction, seven of Pissarro's canvases brought respectable sums. The first Impressionist exhibition was held from March 15 to April 15, in rooms provided by Nadar, 35 Boulevard des Capucines; Pissarro was among the exhibitors. On July 24 his wife gave birth to a son, Felix, who later in life would sign his paintings « Jean Roch ».

1875. Pissarro painted in Pontoise, as did Cézanne, and in Montfoucault. An auction of Impressionist canvases was held but was not overly successful.

1876. In April, the second exhibition of the Impressionists took place at 2 rue Le Peletier; twelve of Pissarro's canvases were included.

1877. The third Impressionist exhibition opened, also in April, at 6 rue Le Peletier, and Pissarro was represented by twenty-two paintings. A second public auction. The New Athens became the café where the artists gathered.

1878. There was an international exposition in Paris. On November 21, Ludovic-Rodolphe Pissarro was born.

1879. The fourth Impressionist show was held from April 10 to May 11, at 28 Avenue of the Opéra; Pissarro exhibited thirty-eight pictures.

1880. April 1 to April 30 saw the fifth group show at 10 rue des Pyramides. This time Pissarro exhibited eleven paintings and etchings. He executed some engravings in collaboration with Degas and Mary Cassatt.

1881. The sixth group show took place at 35 Boulevard des Capucines from April 2 to May 1; Pissarro showed eleven paintings. In Pontoise, Cézanne and Gauguin were his companions. Durand-Ruel's financial situation improved. On August 27, a daughter, Jeanne, was born.

1882. The seventh exhibition of the group, to which Pissarro contributed thirty-six paintings and gouaches. Durand-Ruel was threatened with bankruptcy. Georges Petit organized an international exhibition.

1883. In March, Pissarro had a one-man show at Durand-Ruel's, 251 rue Saint Honoré. He took up residence in Osny, near Pontoise, and worked with Gauguin. Then he left for Les Petites-Dalles and Rouen.

1884. Pissarro abandoned Osny and settled in Eragny, near Gisors, which would be his home for the rest of his life. The Society of Independents was founded; it had the announced goal of organizing a Salon without prizes and without compensation. On August 22, a son, Paul-Emile, was born.

1885. Pissarro made the acquaitance of Theo Van Gogh and of Signac, who introduced him to Seurat. He painted in Eragny, Bazincourt and Gisors.

1886. From the 15th of May to the 15th of June there was the eighth and last exhibition of the group at 1 rue Lafitte. Seurat and Signac participated; Pissarro, who had invited them, sent twenty works of art. He met Vincent Van Gogh, and exhibited at Durand-Ruel's New York gallery. He also adopted the pointillist technique. In New York, Durand-Ruel's exhibition of the best Impressionist canvases at the American Art Association was enormously successful.

1887. Exhibition of pointillist paintings at the Group of XX, in Brussels. Pissarro's son Lucien was now a chromolithographer. There was an international exhibition under the auspices of Georges Petit, to which Pissarro sent some pointillist works.

1888. He abandoned the pointillist technique.

1889. The onset of a chronic infection of the eyes from which Pissarro would suffer until the end of his life. He transformed the attic of his house in Eragny into a large studio. Durand-Ruel purchased a sizable number of his works. An international exposition.

1890. A definitive renunciation of pointillism. Pissarro participated in the exhibition of the XX in Brussels. Lucien Pissarro, who was living in London, was specializing in wood engraving and typography; and Camille Pissarro traveled there to visit him. At the May sale, « Rocquencourt Road » sold for fourteen hundred francs and « Entry into the Village » for twenty-one hundred.

1891. Interested in the work being produced by his son Lucien, Pissarro devoted himself more and more to engraving and lithography, and provided Lucien with drawings which could be translated into engravings.

1892. An impressive Pissarro retrospective at Durand-Ruel's, with a catalogue preface by Georges Lecomte. A loan from Monet enabled him to buy the Eragny house. A trip to London to stay with his son Lucien.

1893. A series of pictures of the Saint Lazare station in Paris. Durand-Ruel journeyed to Eragny and bought twenty-eight thousand six hundred francs' worth of paintings. An exhibition at the Durand-Ruel gallery.

1894. Following the assassination of President Carnot, Pissarro fled to Belgium. The Caillebotte collection was offered to the Louvre. Of the eighteen canvases of Pissarro which were offered, seven were accepted. An exhibition at Durand-Ruel's. Pissarro's interest in lithography increased.

1896. Exhibition at Durand-Ruel's.

1897. The beginning of a series of views of Paris, Pissarro rented a room in the Hotel de Russie, at the corner of the rue Drouot and the Boulevards.

1898. An exhibition at Durand-Ruel's. Pissarro settled in the Hotel of the Louvre in order to paint the Avenue of the Opéra and the Square of the Théâtre Français.

1899. He took up occupancy in an apartment on the rue de Rivoli, from which he could see and paint the Tuileries and the Carrousel.

1901. He went to live in the house of Madame Roland, on the Pont-Neuf, where he painted the bridge, the statue of Henri IV and the quays.

1903. Pissarro took an apartment on the Boulevard Morland. In November, he died of an abscess in the prostate.

BIBLIOGRAPHY

PRINCIPAL MONOGRAPHS AND OTHER WORKS

Duranty: la Nouvelle Peinture (Dentu 1876).

Huysmans J.K.: *l'Art moderne* (Charpentier 1883).

Duret Théodore: *les Peintres impressionistes* (Heymann and Pérois. 1878).

Fénéon Félix: *l'Impressionnisme en 1886* (Léon Vanier. 1886).

Lecomte Georges: *Camille Pissarro* in « les Hommes d'aujourd'hui ». (Léon Vanier 1890).

Castagnary: *Salons.* (Charpentier 1892).

Lecomte Georges: *l'Art impressioniste.* (Chamerot and Renouard 1892).

Geoffroy Gustave: *la Vie artistique* 3rd series. (Dentu 1894).

Mirbeau Octave: *Préface du catalogue de l'exposition de l'œuvre de Camille Pissarro* (Durand-Ruel 1904).

Fontainas André: *Histoire de la Peinture française au XIXᵉ Siècle.* (Mercure de France 1906).

Duret Théodore: *Histoire des peintres impressionnistes.* (Floury 1906).

Meier Graefe Julius: *Impressionnisten: Guys, Manet, Van Gogh, Pissarro, Cézanne* (R. Piper. Munich 1907).

Signac Paul: *d'Eugène Delacroix au Néo-Impressionnisme.* (Floury 1911).

Lecomte Georges: *Camille Pissarro* (Bernheim Jeune. 1922).

Geffroy Gustave: *Claude Monet* (Crès 1922).

Fontainas André and Vauxcelles Louis: *l'Art français de la Révolution à nos jours.* (Sant'Andrea. et L. Marcerou. 1922).

Denis Maurice: *Nouvelles Théories sur l'Art moderne.* (Rouart and Watelin. 1922).

Tabarant A.: *Pissarro* (Rieder 1924).

Focillon H.: *la Peinture aux XIXᵉ et XXᵉ siècles* (Laurens 1928).

Kunstler Ch.: *Paul Emile Pissarro* (Girard and Bunino 1928).

Kunstler Ch. et Basler: *la Peinture indépendante en France* (1929).

Kunstler Ch.: *Camille Pissarro* (Grès 1930).

Uhde W.: *les Impressionnistes* (Phaidon 1937).

Rewald John: *Cézanne* (Albin Michel 1939).

Rewald John: *Camille Pissarro au musée du Louvre* (Marion 1939).

Rewald John: *Histoire de l'Impressionnisme* (Albin Michel 1955).

Lethève Jacques: *Impressionnistes et Symbolistes devant la presse* (Armand Colin 1959).

Rewald John: *Le Post-Impressionnisme* (Albin Michel 1961).

Kunstler Ch.: *Pissarro, villes et campagnes* (Bibliothèque des Arts 1967).

Boulton Alfredo: *Camille Pissarro en Venezuela.* (Caracas. Editorial Arte 1966).

Französische Impressionnisten, Hommage à Durand-Ruel. (Hamburg 1970-71).

Kunstler Ch.: *Pissarro* (Fabbri, Milan, 1973).

WORKS ON ENGRAVING

DELTEIL Loys: *Pissarro, Sisley, Renoir*. Vol. 17. Collection « les Peintres Graveurs illustrés ». Paris 1923.

ROGER-MARX Claude: *Camille Pissarro graveur* (Gallimard 1929).

ROGER-MARX Claude: *la Gravure originale de Monet à nos jours* (Hyperion 1939).

ADHÉMAR Jean: *la Lithographie en France* (Paris 1942).

LARAN Jean: *l'Estampe* (Presses Universitaires de France. 1959).

ROGER-MARX Claude: *la Gravure originale au XIXe siècle* (Somogy 1962).

BERSIER Jean-Eugène: *la Gravure* (Berger-Levrault 1963).

MELOT Michel and LEYMARIE Jean: *les Gravures des Impressionnistes* (Arts et métiers graphiques. 1791).

LETTERS AND CATALOGUES

PISSARRO Ludovic Rodo et VENTURI Lionello: *Camille Pissarro, son Art, son Œuvre*. Editions Paul Rosemberg. Paris 1939. 2 vol. Catalogue raisonné of paintings totaling 1668 items.

PISSARRO Camille: *Lettres à son fils Lucien*. Editions Albin Michel. 1950.

VENTURI Lionello: *les Archives de l'Impressionnisme*.

Durand-Ruel 1939. 2 vol. Letters from Renoir, Monet, Pissarro, Sisley and various documents.

Lettres de Camille Pissarro à Octave Mirbeau 1891-1892.

GACHET Paul: *Lettres impressionnistes*. Grasset. Paris 1957.

ILLUSTRATIONS